A Day in the Life: Rain Forest Animals

Lemur

Anita Ganeri

Heinemann Library
Chicago, IL

www.capstonepub.com
Visit our website to find out
more information about
Heinemann-Raintree books.

To order:

☎ Phone 800-747-4992

💻 Visit www.capstonepub.com
to browse our catalog and order online.

Edited by Nancy Dickmann, Rebecca Rissman, and
Catherine Veitch
Designed by Steve Mead
Picture research by Mica Brancic
Originated by Capstone Global Library
Printed in the United States of America in North Mankato,
Minnesota. 062014 008261RP

16 15 14
10 9 8 7 6 5 4

**Library of Congress Cataloging-in-
Publication Data**
Ganeri, Anita, 1961-
  Lemur / Anita Ganeri.—1st ed.
      p. cm.—(A day in the life. Rain forest animals)
  Includes bibliographical references and index.
  ISBN 978-1-4329-4111-6 (hc)—ISBN 978-1-4329-4122-2
(pb) 1. Lemur (Genus)—Juvenile literature. I. Title.
  QL737.P95G36 2011
  599.8'3—dc22   2010001134

Acknowledgments
We would like to thank the following for permission to
reproduce photographs: Alamy pp. 10 (© Martin Harvey),
20 (© Fotosonline/Peter Kelly); Ardea pp. 6 (M. Watson),
16 (Thomas Marent); Corbis p. 12 (Encyclopedia/© Gallo
Images); FLPA pp. 4, 19, 23 mammal (David Hosking), 15,
23 fossa (Ariadne Van Zandbergen), 17 (Jurgen & Christine
Sohns), 21 (Albert Visage), 22 (Minden Pictures/Thomas
Marent); Photolibrary pp. 5 (John Warburton-Lee
Photography/Nigel Pavitt), 7, 9, 13, 23 tuft (Tips Italia/John
Devries), 11 (Picture Press/ Jurgen & Christine Sohns), 18
(Oxford Scientific (OSF)/David Haring/DUPC); Photoshot
pp. 14, 23 troop (NHPA/Kevin Schafer); Shutterstock p. 23
rain forest (© Szefei).

Cover photograph of a black and white ruffed lemur hanging
upside down in a tree reproduced with permission of Getty
Images (Gallo Images/Martin Harvey).

Back cover photographs of (left) fossa reproduced with
permission of FLPA (Ariadne Van Zandbergen); and
(right) young lemur reproduced with permission of FLPA
(David Hosking).

We would like to thank Michael Bright for his invaluable help
in the preparation of this book.

Contents

Some words are in bold, **like this**. You can find them in the glossary on page 23.

A lemur is a **mammal**.

Many mammals have hairy bodies and feed their babies milk.

indri

There are many different types of lemurs.

The biggest lemur is the indri.

tail

Lemurs have long arms and legs and often have long tails.

Their strong hands and fingers help them to climb trees.

Lemurs have thick fur that can be brown, black, white, or red.

This lemur has **tufts** of fur around its neck.

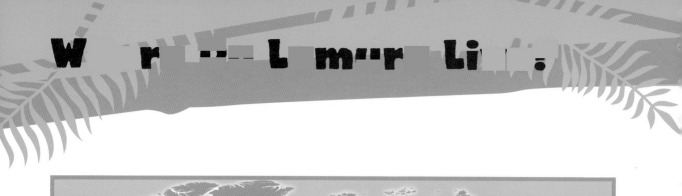

Madagascar

Lemurs live on the island of Madagascar in the Indian Ocean.

Wild lemurs are not found anywhere else on Earth.

8

The lemurs in this book live in the
rain forests in Madagascar.

In a rain forest, it is warm and wet all
year long.

What Do Lemurs Do During the Day?

Many types of lemurs wake up when the sun rises.

They spend the morning moving through the trees looking for food.

In the afternoon, some lemurs like to rest in the sun.

They sit on a branch and stretch their arms out wide.

Lemurs eat fruit, leaves, and seeds.

A lemur also uses its long tongue to reach deep inside flowers for food.

Some lemurs hang upside down from trees to feed.

They hang onto the branches with their feet.

Many lemurs live in groups of up to 20 animals.

A group is called a **troop**.

fossa

Living in a group helps to keep the lemurs safe.

It is easier for an animal such as a **fossa** to attack one lemur rather than a group.

What Does a Lemur Sound Like?

Lemurs make a lot of different sounds.

They wail, scream, snort, yap, and groan.

These sounds help the lemurs to keep in touch with one another.

They also warn other groups of lemurs to stay in their own space.

Where Are Baby Lemurs Born?

Some baby lemurs are born in nests in the treetops.

A female lemur builds the nest out of twigs, leaves, and moss.

baby

During the day, female lemurs carry their babies with them as they look for food.

Baby lemurs cling to their mother's belly or back.

What Does a Lemur Do at Night?

In the evening, lemurs look for more food to eat.

Then they go to sleep on a branch or in a hollow tree.

Some rain forest lemurs look for food at night.

Other lemurs move around from time to time during the day and night.

fur

ear

eye

leg

snout

ruff

tail

Glossary

fossa meat-eating animal that lives in Madagascar

mammal animal that feeds its babies milk. Most mammals have hair or fur.

rain forest thick forest with very tall trees and a lot of rain

troop group of lemurs

tuft bunch of something, such as fur, that grows from the same place

Books

Riley, Joelle. *Ring-Tailed Lemurs.* Minneapolis: Lerner Publications Company, 2009.

Shores, Erika L. *Lemurs: Tree Dwellers.* Mankato, MN: Brigestone Books, 2005.

Websites

www.durrell.org/animals/mammals/redruffed-lemur
www.arkive.org/indri/indri-indri/

Index